Dino Mania

DISCOVERING WHO'S WHO IN THE JURASSIC ZOO

Michael A. DiSpezio

Sterling Publishing Co., Inc.
New York

Acknowledgment

I'd like to recognize the American Museum of Natural History in New York City for filling me with the wonderment of science through their extensive exhibits on dinosaurs and sea life. This museum, like all great learning places, remains a true arena of inspiration. Thank you, Natural History Museum. I'd also like to acknowledge the hard work, talent, and dedication of one of my favorite friends and colleagues, Hazel Chan. I've been fortunate to have Hazel as my editor on quite a few Sterling projects. Extending far beyond catching errors and oversights, Hazel's perceptiveness has been critical to the successful look and feel of these projects. Thank you, Hazel.

Design by Nancy B. Field

Library of Congress Cataloging-in-Publication Data Available

10 9 8 7 6 5 4 3 2 1

Published by Sterling Publishing Co., Inc.
387 Park Avenue South, New York, N.Y. 10016

© 2002 by Michael A. DiSpezio

Distributed in Canada by Sterling Publishing
c/o Canadian Manda Group, One Atlantic Avenue, Suite 105
Toronto, Ontario, Canada M6K 3E7
Distributed in Great Britain and Europe by Chris Lloyd at Orca Book
Services, Stanley House, Fleets Lane, Poole BH15 3AJ, England
Distributed in Australia by Capricorn Link (Australia) Pty. Ltd.
P.O. Box 704, Windsor, NSW 2756 Australia

Sterling ISBN 0-8069-8981-5

Table of Contents

The Journey Begins

Have you ever wished that dinosaurs were still around? Go on. Be honest. You're among friends. If you're like most of us, you probably think it would be really cool to have a real Jurassic Park around the block. Who wouldn't? It sure beats checking out the mall pet store!

Dinosaurs, however, have been dead for millions of years. But don't worry, we won't let that get in the way. We'll bring back those good old days, sort of. *Dino Mania* is packed with all kinds of dinosaur activities, projects, and things to do. So if reading the same facts over and over again is ancient history, here's a chance to do something about it—really *do something* about it.

Plus, we promise not to disappoint you dino-heads either. This book is packed with all sorts of dino-mite information, fun factoids, and trivia quizzes. So turn the page and let your journey begin!

Prehistoric Quiz

Everything you've ever been taught is right. Right? Wrong.

It may not be news to you, but sometimes old (and incorrect) ideas stick around way too long. Want to see what we mean?

Uncover fact from fiction. Take this test about prehistoric times.

TRUE or FALSE?

1. There were no flying dinosaurs.

2. The largest dinosaurs dragged their heavy tails along the ground.

3. *Brontosaurus* was a large plant-eating dinosaur.

4. Even the smallest dinosaur was larger than a person.

5. Dinosaurs did not have feathers.

ANSWER: Would you be surprised to learn that all these statements are false? That's right, every one of them is false. Instead of cluttering up this page with additional facts, you can learn more about each of these statements in the pages that follow.

TIMES, THEY ARE A'CHANGING

Until the mid-1970s, our knowledge of dinosaurs pretty much stayed the same. Sure, there were the occasional new species or an unexpected fossil find, but for the most part, scientists were pretty certain in their knowledge of these extinct beasts. Dinosaurs were written off as slow, cold-blooded, tail-dragging, dimwits that were slightly brighter than the star, *Alpha Centauri*.

Then things changed. Scientists began to reexamine what they thought was the absolute truth. The more they investigated, the more it seemed that dinosaurs were misunderstood. VERY MISUNDERSTOOD.

A Line on the Past

Dinosaurs first appeared on our planet about 250 million years ago. Although it seems like a long time ago, it's a fairly recent event in a planet that's been around for 4500 million years, or 4½ billion years.

To get a feel for the time that the dinosaurs lived on Earth, let's construct this bedroom time line.

You'll Need

Kite string   Ruler
Tape   Washable markers

To Do

1. Cut a length of string that's about 9 feet (or 2.7 m) long. This length will represent the age of the Earth.

2. Stretch the string between opposite walls. Use tape to secure its ends to the wall or floor. Don't forget to pull the string tightly so that it doesn't sag.

3. The far end of the string marks the formation of the Earth. Use your ruler to measure out 1-foot (30-cm) segments from this spot. Identify each length with a mark. According to most scientific theories, the Earth is about 4½ billion years old. If you do a little math, you can figure out that each of the nine string sections equals a period of about 500 million years.

4. Now, let's work with the present. The place where the near end of the string is taped on the floor represents today (as in right now, as in taping a string to the floor).

5. This most recent segment begins 1 foot (30 cm) from the end, or about 500 million years ago. About an inch before this segment starts (544 million years ago) animals developed hard body parts, such as shells, teeth, and bones. Before that, they were mostly mush. Well, not exactly mush, but they had soft body parts that did not survive well in the rocks.

6. Divide the final 1-foot (30-cm) segment in half. This mark represents about 250 million years ago. At this time, dinosaurs first appeared.

7. Make a mark about 1½ inches (4 cm) from the end. This mark identifies 65 million years ago. It's at this point when all dinosaurs became extinct.

8. Now, make one final thin mark right at the tip end of the string. This line needs to be very thin, about the width of a pencil mark. Not a very impressive line. It is this mark, however, that represents total human history!

Prehistoric Seas

Dinosaurs weren't the first prehistoric creatures. In fact, by the time they arrived on the scene, all sorts of cool sea animals had already appeared. Perhaps the best known of these sea creatures were the trilobites (TRY-low-bites). The trilobites were distant relatives of our modern-day crabs and lobsters.

Although trilobites get most of the press, there were other animals in the prehistoric seas. Nautoloids (NAW-toe-loids) were ancient cousins of today's squid. They had a head that was surrounded by tentacles and a body protected by a hard shell. Although they were prehistoric, they shot through the water using jet propulsion. They'd take water into a large opening in their body. Then they'd "lock down" the hatches and squirt out a blast of water. This powerful jet of water propelled the animal in the opposite direction.

JET-PROPELLED CREATURES

Let's make a model that shows jet-propelled movement in the following activity.

You'll Need
Kite string
Straw
Tape
Balloon

To Do

1. Insert a length of kite string through a straw.
2. Stretch the kite string across a room. Tape the ends to the walls so that the string remains tight.
3. Blow up a balloon. Hold the neck so that air doesn't escape.
4. Tape the balloon to the straw.
5. Release the neck of the balloon. As air rushes out through the neck, the balloon rockets off in the opposite direction.

Jet-Propelled Sea Creature

On the Move

Did you know that the ground beneath your feet is constantly shifting? If you're an ordinary human being, you can't feel it. That's because the ground moves ever so slowly.* Ultra-slowly. But it does moves.

This movement of the Earth's crust has been going on for billions of years. In fact, some of the major movements scattered huge landmasses across the globe! Can you guess what was on those landmasses? That's right, dinosaurs! So the dinos actually got a free ride. However it wasn't a very fast or exciting one. The ground probably moved less than a foot during the life of one of these beasts.

At the time the dinosaurs first appeared, the continents didn't look like they do now. Back then, most of the Earth was connected in one giant supercontinent called Pangaea (pan-JEE-uh).

As the Earth's surface rocked and rolled, Pangaea split up into large masses. Over hundreds of millions of years, these pieces shifted into the layout of our present-day landmasses. Dinosaurs didn't have to be alive in order to be carried by the moving crust. The remains of dinosaurs that lived together can now be found an ocean apart!

That's because after the animals died, the landmass split and the dino bones went in opposite directions.

FLIPPING THROUGH HISTORY

If you're like most kids, you've probably created all sorts of flipbook cartoons. You know the type: Line figures that dance across the margin of your history book.

This same type of animation can be used to show the breakup of the Pangaea and the movement of its parts across the globe. Trace or photocopy the key frames that are illustrated here. Use your scissors to carefully trim each box. Assemble a stack of these frames. Frame 1 should be at the bottom of the stack, Frame 6 at the top. As you flip the pages of the stack, you'll see the split up of a supercontinent into its smaller parts. To make the movement appear smooth, you can draw additional "in-between" frames. These frames will show the continent positions and shapes at halfway points between the key frames.

*Unless of course it slips quickly in a movement called an earthquake.

6

3

5

2

4

1

13

Only the Shadow Knows

SILHOUETTE TEST

You know more than you think. In fact, you probably know plenty about prehistoric animals. Do you think you can identify beasts from their silhouettes alone? To find out, take this test. Study each outline and match the shape to its correct name.

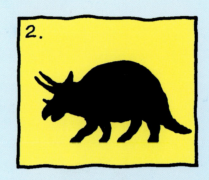
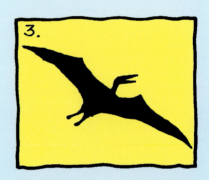

Wooly mammoth   *Stegosaurus*
Dimetrodon   *T. rex*
Pteranodon   *Triceratops*

Answers on page 78.

THINK QUICK

A person who studies dinosaurs and other prehistoric animals is called:

1. Weird
2. A paleontologist
3. Someone with plenty of time on her hands

ANSWER: 2. A paleontologist.

Nice guess. But before you can go on, you'll need to pronounce this winning answer. Read my lips. Scientists who study prehistoric life forms are called pay-lee-on-TOL-o-jists.

The *paleo* in paleontologist comes from the Greek word meaning "long ago." That should make plenty of sense since a paleontologist is someone who studies old things.

That same *paleo* is placed at the beginning of a term that identifies a segment of time (called an era) that occurred just before the time of dinosaurs. The Paleozoic (pay-lee-o-ZOH-ik) Era was an ancient time in which animals and plants first started living on land. It lasted for about 400 million years, making up a little less than 10% of the Earth's total history.

Lay It on Me

Imagine a desk that is buried beneath a mountain of papers, old homework assignments, and an assortment of garbage.

Suppose you started digging down through this mess. The most recent papers would be found at the top of this pile. As you dug deeper, you'd uncover older and older papers. Eventually you might find the lost French assignment from fourth grade—and that *would* be something, since you never actually wrote it!

This same concept of older equals deeper is found in a type of rock called sedimentary (sed-i-MEN-tary) rock. Sedimentary rocks have layers. Like flowers pressed in a book, the dino-traces remain mostly undisturbed and preserved within these rock layers. It's up to the dinosaur hunter to uncover the treasures of these sedimentary rocks!

MAKING LAYERS

Here's a quick modeling activity in which you'll observe the formation of sedimentary layers.

You'll Need

Tall clear plastic drinking glass
Tap water
Spoon
Different colors of sand
   (available at a hobby shop)
Tiny seashells or plastic charms
   (cheap version of fossils)

To Do

1. Fill the glass two-thirds full with water.
2. Add several spoonfuls of pink sand to the water. What happens as the sand enters your mini-ocean?
3. Now add several spoonfuls of green sand. You might wish to drop a "fossil" onto the surface of the sand bottom.
4. Cover the fossil with another layer of sand. Keep creating different colored layers until the water approaches the top of the glass.

Presto, you've just made a model of the formation of sedimentary rock layers!

Who's a Fossil?

Which of the following is not a fossil?

a) Petrified bone

b) Insects trapped in prehistoric tree sap

c) Prehistoric footprints recorded in rock

d) Dinosaur eggshell

e) *T. rex* tooth

f) Wooly mammoth frozen in ice

g) Leaf imprints of a prehistoric fern

h) Fourth-grade math teacher

ANSWER: h) Most likely, your math teacher is the only item on this list that is not a fossil. He's just old. So even though he appears to have gone to high school during the Paleozoic Era, that doesn't count. He's a creature of and in the present.

DEFINITION TIME

A fossil is any trace or remains of a living thing that was alive in the past. Often, fossils are formed when a plant or animal gets buried in the Earth's crust. If this burial is quick, then the rock covering protects the remains from being eaten or destroyed.

← Amber

But not all fossils come from quick burials. Sometimes insects can get trapped in the sticky sap of trees. When this sap hardens, it forms a solid, yellow material called *amber*. Those prehistoric insects, complete with intact wings, are fossils.

Another type of fossil forms when an animal gets stuck and preserved in a block of ice. Although you can't thaw the ice to get a living creature, this frozen tomb can preserve the creature's finest features.

WOOLY ON ICE

Curb Your Dinosaur

Many parts of a dinosaur can form fossils, even its waste. Scientists have a cool (and kind of cryptic) name for fossilized droppings. It's called coprolite (coh-PRO-lite). We're happy to report that the fossil, unlike the fresh material, is not made of dinosaur waste. Coprolite is a hard rock whose appearance depends upon the type of minerals that turned this dinosaur dropping into a rock.

What is the state fossil of Arizona?

a) Petrified wood

b) *Stegosaurus*

c) *T. rex*

d) Coprolite

ANSWER: a) Petrified wood. Wood becomes a rock after a tree dies. The wood gets buried and reacts with the surrounding mud and ash. Minerals seep in and replace the soft parts with rock-hard crystals.

Making a Lasting Impression

A mold is something you can make by:

a) throwing a sandwich behind the couch.

b) pressing a hard object into a lump of clay.

Although both answers are correct, we'll stick with choice b. A mold is an impression of an object.

A cast is the reverse of a mold. It is a copy of the original object that made the impression. If a rock contains a footprint, scientists will fill it with plaster. When it hardens, the plaster becomes a cast of the footprint mold.

CASTING DEPARTMENT

Follow these simple directions to make your own mold and cast.

You'll Need

Modeling clay (worked and softened)

Small plastic bowl

Key

Cooking oil

Protective eye goggles

Non-toxic modeling plaster (ask for this at a hobby or school supply store)

Large mixing bowl

Spoon

Water

To Do

1. Place a lump of modeling clay into a small plastic bowl.
2. Soften and press out the clay into a smooth surface. The clay surface must be soft enough to record an impression of the key.
3. Carefully push the key into the surface of the clay. The impression will be used as a mold.

4. Spread out a thin layer of cooking oil over the surface of the clay (including the impression). This will prevent the hardening plaster from sticking to the clay surface.

5. Put on protective eye goggles. Ask an adult to mix up a solution of modeling plaster following the instructions on the box. Make sure you follow all safety precautions and perform this step in a well-ventilated area.

6. Pour the mixture into the mold, making sure you fill the impression completely. The mixture should extend beyond the impression.

7. When the plaster has hardened, carefully remove the solid cast from the bowl. With a light tap, the cast should fall right out of the bowl.

8. If you wish, use paints to highlight the cast.

Chicken Bone Casts

You can make casts of all sorts of objects, including shells and chicken bones. If you wish to use a bone, have an adult clean all the meat off a chicken thighbone that has been boiled in water.

> **CAUTION:**
> An adult must prepare this bone because it involves using a sharp knife and boiling water.

Back on Track

Walk through your backyard after a soaking rainstorm and what do you make? A mess!

Your weight pushes down onto the muddy soil and creates a record of your travel. Scientists call this pattern of footprints a *trackway*. Like other impressions, these footprints can be filled with plaster and used to produce casts.

HOW BIG WAS BIG BIRD?

Imagine a dinosaur whose body was designed like an ostrich. You can "guesstimate" the head-to-tail length of this two-legged creature by multiplying its footprint length by ten.

Now you do it. Measure the length of the footprint that is stomped onto this page. From this measurement, calculate the length of the animal's body. It's that easy!

Answer on page 78.

FOUR-LEGGED FUN

Dinosaurs that walked on four legs had a different body shape than those that walked on two legs. To get the full length of this type of dino, you have to uncover its shoulder-to-hip length.

The best way to get the shoulder-to-hip length is to look at the trackway. First, you need to tell the front prints from the hind prints. That's easy. The hind prints are larger.

The shoulder-to-hip length is equal to the distance from the hind right footprint to the front left footprint. Since dinosaurs didn't take ballet, the right footprints always stay on the right side of the trackway while the left footprints remain on the left side.

Once you have the shoulder-to-hip length, the rest is basic math. Multiply this measurement by four and you can "guesstimate" the total body length of this animal.

• COOL FACT •

In 1802, a 12-year-old kid found the first dinosaur footprints in North America.

Where in the World?

So you'd like to go fossil hunting? Who wouldn't? Just think of finding a *T. rex* tooth that you could hang above your bed! Or maybe you'd settle for uncovering a *Velociraptor* claw that you could carry in your pocket? Wouldn't that be cool?

But don't get your hopes up too high. Sure, there are plenty of places that have fossil remains, but most of these fossils aren't traces of dinosaurs. They are mostly fossils of animals without backbones, such as shellfish and coral.

If, however, you're lucky enough to explore a place where real dinosaur bones have been uncovered, then that's a different story! But even then, don't expect that your private *T. rex* skeleton is around the next bend. These types of fossil finds are very rare. Only about one dozen *T. rex* skeletons have ever been found!

Check out this map. It shows you all the places where dinosaur fossils were found.

As you can see, the sites at which dinosaur fossils are found are often clumped

together. In the United States, there are several "highways" full of fossils that run north and south along the Rocky Mountains and Great Plains. There's even a set of sites along the Mid-Atlantic States.

Some of the greatest finds, however, were uncovered in the Gobi Desert. The Gobi (Go-bee) is a large, dry region in central China and Mongolia. Southeast Asia and Australia also have sites where many dinosaur fossils have been unearthed! Other dino fossil sites are located in Africa, Europe, and South America.

FINDING FOSSIL LOCATIONS

You can narrow down your search by doing a little library (or Internet) work. If you're looking for dinosaur fossils, search for the location of sedimentary rocks that were formed during the age of these prehistoric beasts. That means finding rocks that are anywhere between about 65 to 250 million years old. For you dino-heads, the Age of Dinosaurs is called the Mesozoic Era (mez-o-ZO-ik).

Allosaurus fragilis

• COOL FACT •

In 1979, a 13-year-old girl found the remains of *Allosaurus fragilis*, a fierce meat-eating dinosaur.

First Find

The first dinosaur bones ever uncovered were thought to come from:

a) sea monsters.

b) very large hamsters.

c) dragons.

ANSWER: c) dragons. Although no one knows for certain, it is believed that the Chinese first discovered dinosaur bones over 2000 years ago! However, since the ancient Chinese did not know about dinosaurs, the bones were thought to be the remains of mythical dragons.

GREAT LIZARDS!

TAKE A NOTE

Do you take good notes? If not, this story may change your habits. The person who first made the connection between petrified bones and extinct reptiles was an Englishman named William Buckland. You've probably never heard of him. That's because he was a terrible note taker. However, from notes, journals, and other people's publications, it appears as if Buckland was the first person to put two and two together. Based upon fossil teeth and a fragment of jawbone, he proposed that huge lizard-like creatures once walked the Earth. That was 1824, and his creature was called *Megalosaurus*, which means "great lizard."

• COOL FACT •

Did you know that the explorers Lewis and Clark probably found dinosaur remains as they explored America? They thought, however, that the petrified 3-foot (1-m) rib bones they found belonged to fish—not long dead reptiles.

MORE ENGLISH

It is 1825. You are Gideon Mantell, an English doctor who likes to collect fossil bones. For several years, you have kept several teeth that are different from any of the other old bones you have found. Although they look exactly like the chompers of a modern-day lizard (called an iguana), they are huge! In fact, the teeth are about twenty times larger than the teeth of any living iguana.

Like Buckland, you put two and two together (actually you multiply the length of a living iguana by twenty) and come up with the size for a huge lizard. You call the prehistoric animal *Iguanodon*, or "iguana-tooth." A short time later, *Iguanodon* and *Megalosaurus* are placed in a brand-new group of animals called dinosaurs.

THE TRUTH ABOUT *IGUANODON*

The fossil spike that was part of the *Iguanodon* skeleton was at first thought to be a horn. So, like the horn of a rhinoceros, it was placed on the snout of the animal. Things change. It was later discovered that this spike wasn't a horn. Instead, it was an extension of the thumb. Using the "I'll poke your eye out" defense system, *Iguanodon* protected itself against nasty predators of its time.

Puzzling Pieces

Most of what we know about dinosaurs comes from their skeletal remains. That's because it's just bones that are usually left behind. The dino's softer body parts decayed a long time ago.

Most fossil skeletons are not complete. In fact, some species of dinosaurs are known only from a single skull or other small part of the skeleton. That's it. The only evidence for the existence of an entire species may be one bone. From this limited information, however, scientists are able to make "best guesses" about the animal's size, shape, appearance, and lifestyle.

SAVE THIS BOOK

Make a photocopy of this incomplete skeleton of a *Triceratops*. Then draw in the missing bones based upon what you know about animal skeletons.

Answer on page 78.

Putting It All Together

Here's a complete skeleton of *T. rex* in pieces. Do you think you can put it together?

Make a copy of page 31. If you want a more permanent copy of your work, use a glue stick to secure your assembled pieces onto a backing of heavy-stock paper.

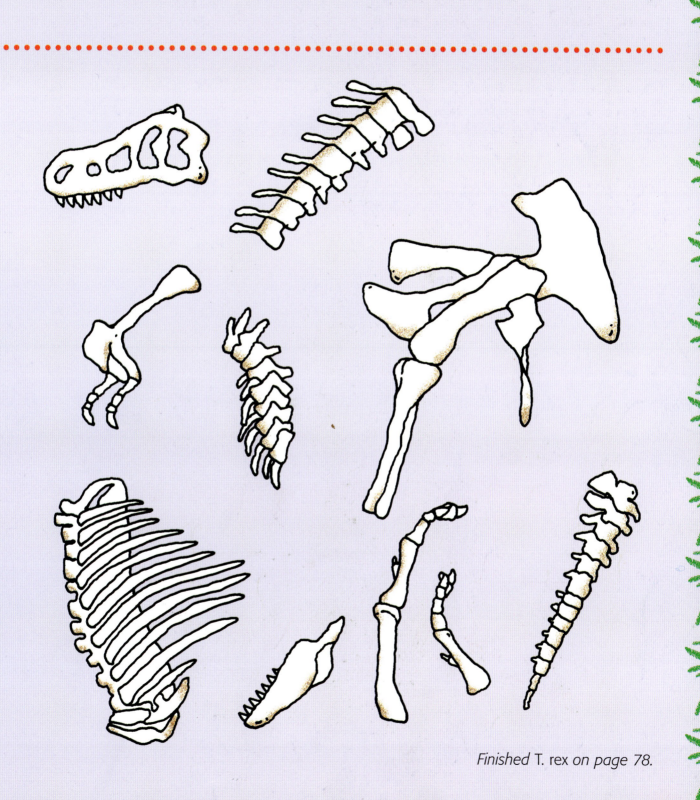

Finished T. rex on page 78.

Being a Reptile

Dinosaurs were reptiles. Like all reptiles, they had certain features. Touch a snake or lizard and you'll observe that the skin is dry. Likewise, the dinosaurs had dry skin. They also had a body covering of scales, similar to those found on today's lizards and snakes.

Like modern-day reptiles, dinosaurs also laid eggs that were covered by a hard shell. These shells were waterproof so that any liquid that was stored within the egg stayed there. This wet environment prevented anything on the inside (such as a developing *Apatosaurus*) from drying out.

EGG SENSE

Eggshells are thin in order to:
a) save on materials.
b) impress people with their strength.
c) allow gases into and out of the egg.

ANSWER: c) Eggshells need to be thin in order to allow gases to pass into and out of the egg. If the shells were thick, they'd get in the way of oxygen flow. Without an oxygen supply, the developing critter would suffocate. So even though a thicker shell would offer more protection, it would prevent the necessary exchange of gases.

EGG-STRA STRENGTH

Although they may not appear it, eggs are sturdy objects. The strength of an egg comes from its round shape. Like the dome on a sports arena, this shape supports itself. So when a force pushes down on it, the shape braces together and resists crumbling.

You'll Need

Several raw eggs
An adult
Assortment of books

To Do

1. Have an adult poke a hole in a chicken egg and drain its liquid contents.
2. Don't let the adult go! Have him cut the shell in half to make two eggshell domes. Before he leaves, have him create two more eggshell domes.
3. Carefully clean, rinse, and dry the shell halves.
4. Place the eggshell domes at the corners of an imaginary rectangle.
5. Place a book on these eggshell domes. Did the domes crush or did they support the weight of the book?
6. Continue stacking the books until the domes give way. You can find out how much weight they supported by weighing the books on a bathroom scale.

Reptiles That Rule

Ruling lizards were the "big kahunas" of the prehistoric past. They included:

Dinosaurs
Crocodiles
Pterosaurs
Birds

Actually, none of these animals were actual lizards. Therefore, the term "ruling lizards" is a slight fib. To clear up this misconception, scientists prefer to call them Archosaurs (Ark-o-saws).

HOLE IN THE HEAD?

To be considered a ruling lizard, you need to have a hole in your head. Actually, you needed four holes: Two on each side. These holes were natural spaces in the skull. They were located behind the eye sockets. Dinos, crocodiles, pterosaurs, and birds all have this distinguishing characteristic.

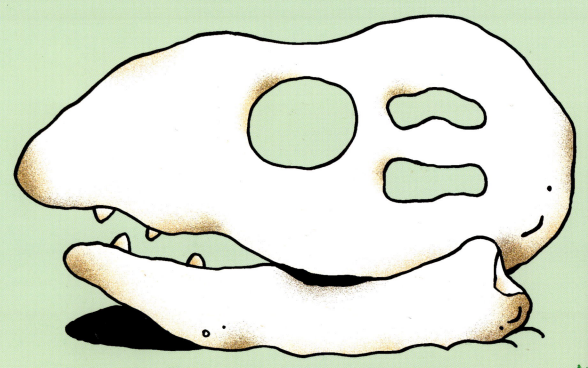

EQUAL TIME FOR CROCS!

Since crocodiles lived side-by-side with dinosaurs (and out-survived them) we should say a few kind words on their behalf.

At the end of the Age of Dinosaurs, gigantic crocodiles ruled the swamps. No one argued with a prehistoric croc, not even a *T. rex*. That's because some ancient crocodiles were longer than a school bus!

Deinosuchus (Di-no-SOO-kus) was a 40-foot-long (12-m) giant that lived in the swamps of North America. Its favorite food was probably very large turtles.

When the dinosaurs became extinct, some of the crocodile species survived. It's nice to know that *Deinosuchus* was not one of them. Only the smaller crocodiles lived and evolved into our present-day species.

• MODERN MONSTERS •

A modern-day saltwater crocodile that lives in the Indian Ocean can grow up to 20 feet (6 m) in length!

Obtaining a Dinosaur ID

Ever wonder why pterosaurs and pterodactyls aren't considered real dinosaurs? Ask a parent or a teacher and they'll ramble off something like, "Dinosaurs didn't fly."

The "doesn't fly" reason doesn't fly. That's because some dinosaurs did fly. And not only did they fly, but these certified A-1 dinosaurs had feathers as well!

What makes a dinosaur different from other ruling lizards is their bone structure. Therefore, classifying something as a dinosaur must be based on the remains of its skeleton.

For you dino-heads, here are a couple of those special bone structures that make a dinosaur different from other Archosaurs:

Special type of hip socket
Ridges on certain bones

Not very exciting, are they? To the paleontologist, however, these features are hair raising! That's because they can easily be used to identify dinosaurs and that's what counts. By study-ing a fossil skeleton, a scientist can get "proof positive" that an animal was or was not a dinosaur.

DON'T BELIEVE EVERYTHING YOU HEAR!

Fossil skeletons of *Confuciusornis* (kon-FYOO-shis-OR-nis) are very common finds. From its bones, we know that it was a dinosaur. Plus, it was covered with feathers. Double plus, it was an active flier! So when someone tells you dinosaurs didn't fly, tell them about *Confuciusornis*!

Ptero in the Sky

Look up in the sky. Is it a bird? Is it a plane? No, it's a prehistoric flying reptile!

At the beginning of the Age of Dinosaurs, a special group of reptiles evolved into airborne predators. These animals were called pterosaurs (TERAH-saws).

Although they looked the part, pterosaurs were not dinosaurs. They did not have the necessary bone structures needed to be classified as a dinosaur.

TAKE THIS PTERROR-ABLE TEST

True or False?

1. Pterosaurs evolved into today's birds.
2. Pterosaurs were gliders, not active fliers.
3. Flying reptiles first appeared at the end of the Age of Dinosaurs.

1. False. Pterosaurs did not evolve into birds. These flying reptiles formed their own group that was different from both dinosaurs and birds.

Pterosaurs did not evolve into anything. This line died off. When the dinosaurs were wiped out 65 million years ago, so went the pterosaurs.

2. False. Pterosaurs *were* active fliers. Like bats, birds, and insects, these animals could fly. They flapped their wings and got the lift needed for flying. The wings of pterosaurs were similar to bat wings. They were formed by skin that was stretched between the long slender (and highly adapted) finger bones.

3. False. Although it might seem logical that flight was a very special ability that required extra time to develop, it wasn't. The fossil record shows that pterosaurs appeared at about the same time as the first land-walking dinosaurs. At this time, the mammals also made their first appearance—thank you very much.

Impress An Adult!

The *ptero* in pterosaur has nothing to do with the fear that these flying predators would have instilled in helpless prey. Ptera is Latin for "wing." Put the words together and you get *winged lizard*. Not a very terrible tale at all.

OF PTEROSAURS, PTERODACTYLS, AND *PTERANODONS*

Pterosaurs are a large and varied group of flying reptiles. One subgroup of the pterosaurs was the pterodactyls (Terra-DAK-tols). The pterodactyls were the most familiar of these flying reptiles. They had sleek bodies and little or no tail. The pterodactyls included giant species such as *Pteranodon.* This awesome flier had a wingspan the size of a small plane.

Lizard Legs

Check out modern-day lizards. They look like dinosaurs, don't they? In fact, back in the 1950s, lizards were often "dressed up" as dinos for starring roles in science fiction movies.

However, this similarity isn't as strong as you might imagine. Lizards have legs that stick out from the animal's side. This isn't the best arrangement for running. When a lizard moves, it wastes time and energy as its body rocks back and forth.

Unlike lizards, dinosaurs have legs that go straight down from the underside of the body. With knees directly below hips, the limbs have much freer movement. This allowed dinosaurs to move quickly when they had to.

ARTY CONNECTION

Use a lump of modeling clay to show the difference between lizards and dinosaurs. Check out these two drawings. Contrast the placement of the legs. Then build your own version of a lizard and a dinosaur highlighting the difference in stance.

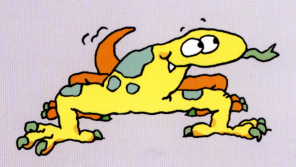

WHEN BEING HIP REALLY MATTERS

What makes a lizard hip?

a) Cool sunglasses.

b) Eating sushi.

c) Bones that extend from the pelvis.

ANSWER: c) You guessed it. It's that old bone thing again. A lizard hip (or pelvis to you skeletal heads) has parts that extend into the belly. The hip also has parts that extend toward the tail.

Why bother with hip bones? A good question. Scientists use the shape of the hip to place dinosaurs into one of two major groups: Lizard-hipped dinos and bird-hipped dinos. The lizard-hipped dinos have a hip that looks like the pelvis of modern-day lizards. The bird-hipped dinos have a hip that looks like the pelvis found in modern-day birds. The bird hip lacks a bone that pushes into the belly of the animal. Without this bone, there is more room for digesting food. This extra room is necessary because the bird-hipped dinos eat an incredible number of plant leaves.

Lizard-hipped Dinos

Gather your art materials because it's time to construct a mobile. This time, however, you won't have seashells hanging from coat hangers. Instead, your mobile will display the groups of lizard-hipped dinos.

BUILD A MOBILE

You'll use cutout dinosaur shapes to construct a hanging model of the classification of lizard-hipped dinosaurs.

You'll Need
Scissors
Glue
Heavy-stock paper
String
Tape
Straws

To Do

1. Make a color copy of the lizard-hipped dinosaurs on these next few pages.
2. Use scissors to carefully cut out the shape of each copied dinosaur.
3. Paste each copy cutout on a backing of heavy-stock paper. On the backing write the name of the dinosaur and the name of the group to which it belongs. The information is beneath each dinosaur.
4. Cut eight pieces of string, each about $1/2$-foot (15-cm) long.
5. Use tape to attach one string to each of the two straws. The end of each string must be attached to the center of the straw.
6. Use tape to attach each of the remaining six strings to each of the six cards. One end of each string should be taped to the middle of each card's upper edge.
7. Assemble the mobile by attaching the free end of the early plant-eaters string to one end of a straw.
8. In the same fashion, attach the long-necked plant-eaters to the opposite end of the same straw.
9. Attach the meat-eater card to the center of this straw.
10. Attach the string from the other straw to the meat-eater card.
11. As you did in steps 7, 8, and 9, attach the small meat-eaters, terrible-clawed dinosaurs, and large meat-eaters to this second straw. The order doesn't matter. Just remember to position two cards at the ends of the straw and the third card in its center.
12. Hang the mobile by the free end of the topmost string.

All the dinos shown on this mobile have lizard hips! The three groups that hang from the meat-eater card were all predators. The other two groups ate only plants.

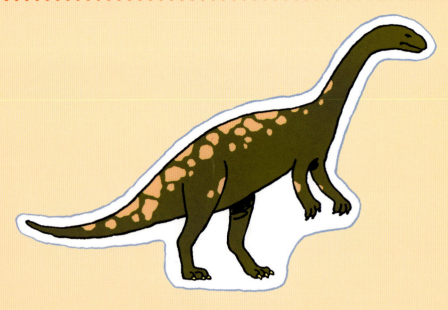

Dinosaur: *Plateosaurus*
Early plant-eaters: Prosauropods

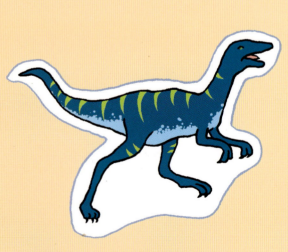

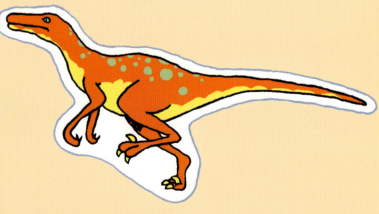

Dinosaur: *Velociraptor*
Terrible-clawed dinosaurs: Deinonychosaurs

Dinosaur: *Compsognathus*
Small meat-eaters: Coelurosaurs

MEAT EATERS

Dinosaur: *Apatosaurus*
Long-necked plant-eaters: Sauropods

Dinosaur: *Allosaurus*
Large meat-eaters: Carnosaurs

Bird-hipped Dinos

Do you like to eat vegetables? Well, neither did many of the lizard-hipped species you saw on the previous page. The bird-hipped dinosaurs, however, were "hip" to eating plants. All were herbivores.

As you learned, bird hips don't extend into the belly. This gives the animal extra room for digesting leaves, branches, and twigs. These animals have another bird-like adaptation. Perhaps you've heard of it? It's called a beak.

MAKE IT A DOUBLE

You'll Need
Scissors
Glue
Heavy-stock paper
String
Tape
Straws

BIRD FOOTED

1. Make a color copy of the bird-hipped dinosaurs illustrated on these next few pages.
2. Use scissors to carefully cut out the shape of each copied dinosaur.
3. Paste each cutout on a backing of heavy-stock paper. On this backing, write the name of the dinosaur and the name of the group to which it belongs. The information is given beneath each animal.
4. Cut eight pieces of string, each about 1/2-foot (15-cm) long.
5. Attach one segment of string to the center top (balance point) of each cutout shape.
6. Use tape to attach one string to the center of the top straw.
7. From this top straw, attach the strings to the plated dinosaurs, armored dinosaurs, bird-footed dinos, and horned dinosaurs. Hang the bird-footed cutout closest to the center of the straw.
8. Cut the second straw in half. Use a piece of string to attach the top center of this straw to the bottom of the bird-footed cutout.
9. Attach the thick-headed dinosaurs and the duck-billed dinosaurs to opposite ends of this shortened straw.
10. Hang the mobile by the free end of the topmost string. You'll most likely have to shift the positions of strings to produce the best balance. As you'll see, all of the dinos shown on this mobile have bird hips! The two groups that hang from the bird-footed card share foot features that are not found in the other three groups.

BIRD-HIPPED FACTS

1. The name *Stegosaurus* means "roofed lizard." As you probably guessed, this name refers to the two rows of plates that ran along the spine of this plant-eating dinosaur.
2. When scientists first discovered duck-billed dinosaurs, they thought that these animals did not have teeth. Things change. After studying more duck-billed skulls, scientists discovered that these animals had hundreds of teeth packed into the back of their bill-like mouth. As these teeth wore out, new ones grew in to take their place!
3. Armored dinosaurs didn't have a solid suit of armor. Instead, they had hundreds of bony plates. These plates were attached side-by-side in the animal's thick hide.

Dinosaur: *Triceratops*
Horned dinosaurs: Ceratopians

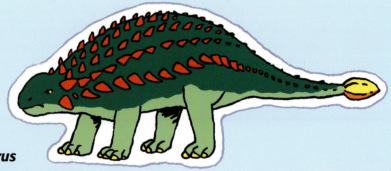

Dinosaur: *Ankylosaurus*
Armored dinosaurs: Ankylosaurs

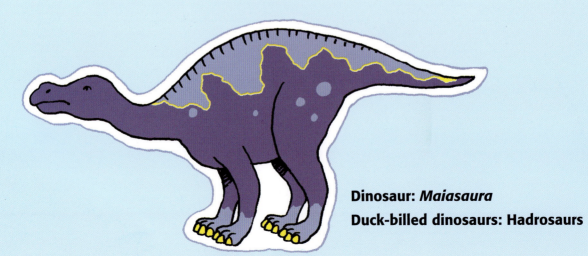

Dinosaur: *Maiasaura*
Duck-billed dinosaurs: Hadrosaurs

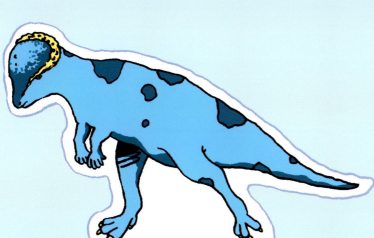

BIRD FOOTED

Dinosaur: *Stegoceras*
Thick-headed dinosaurs: Pachycephalosaurs

Dinosaur: *Stegosaurus*
Plated dinosaurs: Stegosaurs

The Bird Connection

Which of the following two statements is true?

Birds are modern-day dinosaurs.
Birds are not modern-day dinosaurs.

ANSWER: The absolute, definitive answer is that *both* statements are true. It all depends upon how you define a dinosaur. But even if you don't believe that birds are true dinosaurs, their connection to these extinct animals seems stronger than ever.

DINOS ON THE WING

Compare the skeletons of small dinosaurs with those of the earliest birds and what do you find? Similarities. In fact, these skeletons are so alike that they are difficult to tell apart. It's the covering of streamlined feathers used in flying, however, that is the giveaway.

ALL WET

Let's turn back the clock about 80 million years. At this time, there is a feathered friend chasing fish. Its name is *Hesperonis* (HES-pe-RO-nis). Like a modern-day penguin, *Hesperonis* could not fly. Most of its life was spent floating in the ocean. In fact, technically it could be considered a sea dweller.

How can that be? Weren't we taught that dinosaurs had to be land dwellers? Anything that lived mostly in water or in the air couldn't be a dinosaur. Right? Wrong.

It's another one of those misconceptions. Although almost all dinosaurs lived on land, a few took to the air or lived most of their lives on the sea surface. Tell your teacher that it's the bone structure that makes something a dino, not where it lives.

Hesperonis

FEATHERED FRIENDS

Prehistoric birds weren't the only group of dinosaurs that had feathers. Feathers were probably found on all sorts of meat-eating dinosaurs, including raptors and tyrant dinosaurs.

Feathers were a body covering that kept in heat. Baby dinosaurs were covered with feathers to help keep them warm. In some species, this fluffy covering resembled the flight feathers of modern-day birds. Mostly, however, it was a covering of fluffy feathers like those found on ducklings.

Ancient Wing Fliers

The oldest known bird is called *Archaeopteryx* (AHR-kee-OP-ter-iks). As you might imagine, its odd-sounding name translates into something meaningful. It's Latin for "ancient wing."

Archaeopteryx kept some features of the dinosaurs from which it evolved. Like the dinos before, it had teeth, clawed hands, and a long bony tail. It also had characteristics of our modern-day birds: Feathers, a wishbone, and a very bird-like hip.

Although the last *Archaeopteryx* died about 150 million years ago, the legacy of these winged fliers lives on. In fact, we're going to celebrate their "sky's the limit" lifestyle by building a high-flying glider. If you and your friends construct several of these fliers, you can race them in the park. As they glide overhead, it's easy to pretend it's still the age of dinosaurs. You can even videotape the gliders as they streak across your version of a Jurassic public park.

ANCIENT WING GLIDER

To build this glider, get a piece of thin plastic foam material. Try your local butcher shop or grocery store. These places should have foam trays that can be cut down to size. You can also check out a hobby or craft store. Either place will have stock foam material that you can cut into your ancient flying bird.

Materials

Scissors
Thin sheet of plastic foam (from meat tray)
Markers
Tape
Small coin

To Do

1. Photocopy the page with the dino's body, tail, and wings. Cut out the three pieces and trace each outline on a flat sheet of plastic foam.
2. Carefully cut these three pieces from the foam sheet. Don't forget to cut the slots for the wings and tail.
3. Use markers to decorate and color these parts.
4. Insert the wings into the body. Attach the tail to the back body slot.
5. Tape a small coin onto the nose of the glider.
6. Supporting it at the midsection, gently toss the glider.

Archaeopteryx

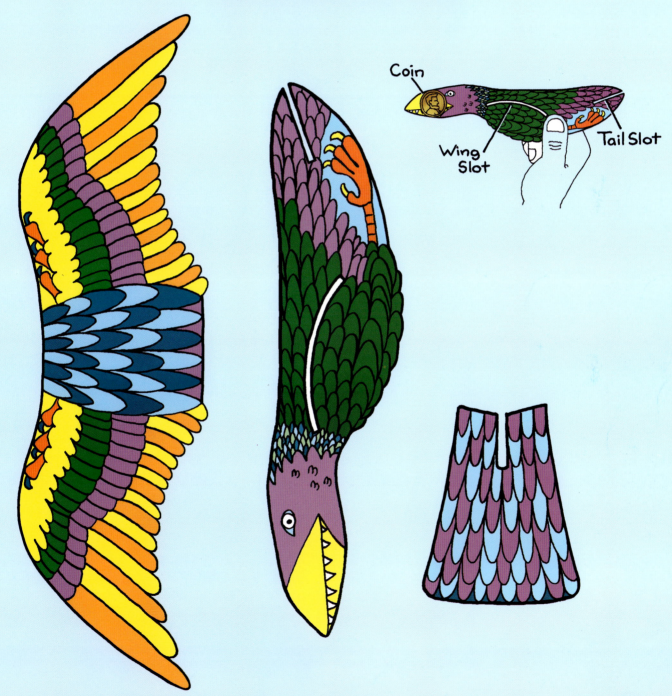

Coin

Wing Slot

Tail Slot

Name Game

Check out the left-hand list of Latin and Greek terms that are used to name dinosaurs. The right-hand list is what those terms mean in English.

a	without	*ornitho*	bird
acro	high	*pachy*	thick
allo	strange	*ped, pod*	foot
alti	high	*pro*	first
ankylo	fused	*ptero*	winged
apato	deceptive	*quadri*	four
bi	two	*raptor*	thief
brachio	arm	*rex*	king
brachy	short	*rhino*	nose
bronto	thunder	*saurus*	lizard
carno	meat	*stego*	roofed
cephlo	head	*thero*	beast
cera	horn	*tri*	three
coelo	hollow	*tyranno*	tyrant
dactyl	finger	*veloci*	speedy
deino	terrible		
derm	skin		
di	two		
don	tooth		
gnathus	jaw		
hadro	sturdy		
hetero	mixed		
mega	huge		
mono	single		
nycho	clawed		

PUTTING IT TOGETHER

Use this list to assemble the "official" name for each of the dinosaurs described below:

1. Tyrant reptile king
2. Thick-headed lizard
3. Speedy thief
4. Terrible-clawed lizard

Answers on page 78.

A DINOSAUR BY ANY OTHER NAME

The word "dinosaur" was made up in 1842 by Professor Richard Owen, a British anatomy expert. He said that these animals belonged to a special bunch of extinct reptiles. To Owen, the word dinosaur meant "fearfully great lizard."

Upscale Art

Have you ever seen a sidewalk artist? You know the type—an artist who sketches a cool copy of some famous painting on the sidewalk? If so, perhaps you know that before they start drawing the actual painting, they lay down a grid of horizontal and vertical lines. The grid forms a pattern of squares that divides the sidewalk canvas into smaller boxes. These squares are used as a reference for copying from the original image, which also has a grid over it.

STARTING SMALL

For our first model, we'll use one of the smallest dinosaurs. Its name is *Compsognathus* (KOMP-so-nah-thus) and it stood about 14 inches (36 cm) tall. This chicken-sized predator had a slender neck and a narrow jaw that was packed with curved, sharp teeth. Its favorite foods probably included insects, other small reptiles, and small mammals.

You'll Need
Large sheet of drawing paper
    (about 20 inches × 30 inches
    /51 cm × 76 cm from an art
    supply store)
Pencil
Ruler
Crayons or markers

To Do

1. Use your pencil and ruler to draw a grid onto a sheet of plain paper. Each of the lines should be separated by exactly 2 inches (5 cm). Make fourteen columns and eight rows of boxes. Your grid should measure out to 28 inches × 16 inches (71 cm × 41 cm).

2. Check out our image of *Compsognathus*. The boxes can be identified by columns (letters) and rows (numbers).

3. Concentrate on one box at a time. See where the dinosaur outline meets the sides of the box. Copy this pattern onto the corresponding box on your piece of paper.

4. Continue your drawing in box-by-box steps. Don't forget to use the box numbers and letters as a reference.

5. When you're done, color in your dinosaur. You will have created a full-size drawing of a *Compsognathus*. You will also have learned a cool copying technique!

Sidewalk Sketch

Now that you know the technique, don't let it go to your head. Instead, let it go to the head of a *T. rex*. Here's your chance to draw an accurate full-size picture of a dinosaur head.

You'll Need

Playground surface that can get "chalked up"

Large pieces of colored chalk

A friend

Yard stick

Kite string

To Do

1. First, make a grid. All the lines in this sidewalk version should be 2 feet (about ½ m) apart.
2. Working with a friend, draw the edge of your rectangular sidewalk canvas. The dimensions should be 6 feet × 8 feet (1.8 m × 2.4 m).

HINT: To make your lines straighter, choose a sidewalk surface that has a rectangular pattern of marked lines, ridges, or cuts from which you can base your marks and angles.

3. Use your yardstick to place a mark at 2-foot (½-m) spaces along all four sides of your rectangle.
4. Pull the kite string tightly across opposite sides. Use it as a guide to draw a straight chalk line across opposite sides at each of the 2-foot (½-m) marks. Continue until the entire grid is complete.

Paper Version

If you don't have a sidewalk handy, you can always create a crayon and paper version of this *T. rex*. Tape the backs of as many drawing sheets as you need together to make your own oversized canvas. The rest remains the same.

It's a Snap

Instead of drawing the chalk line, you can snap chalk dust onto the ground. Simply rub your chalk across the length of your kite string. Pull the chalked string tightly across opposite sides, matching each side of the 2-foot (½-m) mark. Pick up the middle of the string and let it snap against the ground. The impact will leave a chalk record that you can use as a grid line.

Monstrous Proportions

Are you ready for the biggest project of 'em all? Great, because you're about to redefine the envelope of scale drawings. Your subject is a HUGE star who played the bad guy (or bad gal) in *Jurassic Park 3*. Its name is *Spinosaurus*.

Get your friends together. This project will require teamwork to create a grid that is over 40 feet (12 m) long and 20 feet (6 m) tall. Of course, you'll need plenty of chalk—and that's just for the outline!

Like the *Spinosaurus*, the grid squares will be big. Follow the instructions in Sidewalk Sketch (pages 60–61) for making the grids, but for this sketch our sidewalk boxes will be 3 feet × 3 feet (1 m × 1 m). Although the larger boxes lose some of the finer details, they are needed for creating large murals.

• COOL FACT •

The sail on the back of *Spinosaurus* was most likely used to help control the animal's temperature. No, it didn't fan itself with this body part. Learn more about how this sail works on page 67.

Hot-blooded Changes

Feel your forehead. Does it feel warm? It should. If not, then I might be talking to myself.

The warmth you feel is a sign that you are a warm-blooded animal. Like all other warm-blooded animals, you have a very efficient body chemistry that makes you fast, quick, and intelligent. To insure these benefits, your body has a built-in thermostat that keeps you at that ideal temperature of 98.6°F (37°C for you metric types).

In contrast, cold-blooded animals have a body chemistry that depends upon the surroundings. Since they don't maintain a constant warm temperature, their body chemistry changes with the weather. When it's hot, they're hot (and their chemistry is cooking). When the temperature drops, everything drops and their reactions slow. This results in an animal that is generally not very quick.

TURNING UP THE HEAT

At one time, almost all scientists believed that dinosaurs were very similar to today's reptiles. Like turtles and lizards, dinosaurs were thought to be cold-blooded. And if dinos were cold-blooded, it was logical to think of them as dull, tail-dragging slow-pokes. It was nothing personal against dinosaurs. It just made sense.

In the 1970s, scientists took a closer look. Many of the fossil bones

had structures that were found in warm-blooded animals. How could this be?

As they examined more fossils, a new picture began to emerge. Dinos appeared to have a body chemistry closer to warm-blooded birds than to cold-blooded lizards.

Many scientists used this warm-blooded chemistry to rethink the characteristics of these extinct animals. Almost overnight, the textbooks needed to be rewritten.

Dinos were no longer clumsy. They were agile. They weren't slow. They were fast. Even the dimwitted didn't seem so dumb after all. Some species were thought to be intelligent.

These days, there's evidence for both a warm-blooded and cold-blooded body chemistry. Many scientists now believe that the dinosaurs were not truly warm-blooded, but they weren't completely cold-blooded either. They had a middle-of-the-road approach to body temperature.

Keeping Cool

It doesn't matter whether you're hot-blooded or cold-blooded, you need to stay cool in the summertime. Too much heat is a killer, literally.

Dinosaurs and other extinct animals had cool-looking structures for giving off excess heat. Remember the *Stegosaurus*? This dinosaur had a double row of triangular plates that ran along its back. Although they could have helped in defense, scientists believe that these structures were radiators!

When *Stegosaurus* heated up, the body heat went to the plates. This extra heat was radiated from the plates into the surrounding air. This cooled the animal, protecting it from the overheating effects of sunlight.

The plates could also work in reverse. Aimed into the sunlight, they would heat up. The captured heat would be sent around the body and used to keep the whole animal warm.

Dimetrodon was not a dinosaur. It was an ancient reptile that may have been an early ancestor of mammals.

COOLING OFF

By performing this experiment, you can see how a sail or plate helped cool off an animal.

You'll Need
Two large plastic foam cups

Warm water

Thermometer

Scissors

Ruler

Aluminum foil

> **CAUTION:**
> To prevent possible burns, have an adult fill the cups with lukewarm water. Do *not* use hot water.

To Do
1. Fill both cups with warm water.
2. Use a thermometer to measure the temperature of the water.
3. Cut five strips of aluminum foil in the shape of a 1-foot (30-cm) ruler.
4. Place the strips halfway into one of the cups.
5. Place both cups in a breeze or light wind for 15 minutes.
6. Measure the temperature again. Which cup cooled quickest? Why?

Result on page 78.

Head Games

Match the picture of the dinosaur's head with its description. *The answers are on page 78.*

Stegoceras (STEG-oh-sear-az)

This dinosaur had a skull bone thicker than a textbook! This thickened bone worked like a shock absorber. *Stegoceras* would smash heads with other members of its herd. The champion of the duel might become the herd leader.

Parasaurolophus (PAIR-ah-sawr-AHL-uh-fus)

This duck-billed dinosaur had a huge tube that ran along the top of its head. Extending from the back of the skull, the tube contained hollow passageways. Scientists think that these chambers were used to make and amplify sounds.

Brachiosaurus (BRAK-ee-uh-SAWR-us)

This dinosaur had nostrils that were located at the top of its head (like the blowhole of a whale). Scientists first thought that this placement allowed the dino to use its breathing hole like a snorkel. Now, some scientists think this odd placement of the nostrils allowed the dino to keep chewing as it breathed. Others think that the placement helped cool off the brain with a nearby flow of cool air.

Dilophosaurus (Dye-LO-fuh-SAWR-us)

This fierce meat-eater had two half-moon crests located on the top of its head. Scientists think that these crests were used to attract mates. They might have also been used to announce that it was "King of the Hill."

Camarasaurus (KAM-ah-ra-SAW-rus)

This dinosaur had a small head with many teeth. For years, scientists placed this head on the wrong dinosaur body! The mix-up was even given its own name, *Brontosaurus*. But as scientists studied what they had put together, they realized their mistake. The head belonged to a totally different long-necked dinosaur called a *Camarasaurus*. The headless body was soon identified as belonging to an *Apatosaurus*. Although the heads are now on the right body, the confusion still exists. Even today, people incorrectly refer to an *Apatosaurus* as a *Brontosaurus*!

Triceratops (try-SER-ah-tops)

The name of this dinosaur means "three-horns." These horns were great weapons of defense and could protect this plant-eater from predators such as the *T. rex*. *Triceratops* had a beak with teeth that could tear into plants.

Holding Your Tail High

For years, scientists thought that a dinosaur's tail was a drag, literally. Everyone believed that the animal's body couldn't support this huge and heavy hind part. So it seemed to make sense that the animals dragged tails behind them. It wasn't a very majestic image, but it was a practical one that obeyed the law of gravity.

Then scientists took another look at tail dragging and the growing pile of evidence against it.

Evidence #1

Dinos appeared to be fast-moving runners. Tail dragging was not an acceptable behavior for the dino-on-the-go. Imagine a dinosaur running through the jungle dragging its tail along the ground. Ouch, that hurts! Sharp rocks. Ouch!

Evidence #2

Many of the long-tailed species also had long necks or big heads. The tail may have been a way of balancing the front part of its body. Otherwise, the animal's long neck might tip the body over.

Evidence #3

Something was missing. Although there were plenty of footprint fossils, there were no "tail print" fossils. If a tail dragged along the ground, it should have cut a groove in the trackways.

A BALANCING ACT

Let's test out Evidence #2 ourselves. We'll model our dinosaur after the *Brachiosaurus*. It was a huge plant-eater that weighed as much as ten elephants. The *brachio* part of its name means "arms," which refers to its huge front limbs. From head to tail tip, it was about 90 feet (27 m) long.

You need:

Modeling clay
Long piece of uncooked pasta

1. Shape a lump of modeling clay into the body form of a *Brachiosaurus*. Try to copy the exact shape as the illustration shown above, with one exception: Don't include the animal's tail section.
2. To keep the neck from sagging, insert a supportive piece of pasta. Does your model balance?
3. Now add the tail. Make sure to keep the tail horizontal to the ground. If needed, use a piece of pasta to support it.

Colorful Characters

Most dinosaurs were:

a) Gray

b) Brown

c) Paisley

d) No one knows for certain

ANSWER: d) That's right. It's another of those whatever-suits-you-best answers. No one knows for certain the color of a dinosaur's birthday suit.

Skin and scales don't fossilize well. So although we can find the bones of a dinosaur's remains, it's unlikely that we can recover that animal's outermost covering. And even if we did, the color of these remains would most likely have faded out.

That leaves the coloring scheme to the artist. Years ago, the best-known dinosaur artists preferred to paint their beasts in dull shades of brown, green, and gray. It was not very exciting evening wear, but it was thought to be practical.

To match the more recent image of a fast-moving dinosaur, artists now paint these beasts in a kind of an active-wear color scheme. No longer are dinosaurs limited to drab and boring colors. Today's dinos are outfitted in all sorts of colors and patterns.

IT'S A JUNGLE OUT THERE

Turn the page. As you can see, the next spread is a jungle. It's a wild pattern—an ideal environment for hiding some animals. Check out this activity and you'll see how an animal's covering can protect it from being spotted.

You'll Need
Paper
Scissors
Different-colored markers

To Do
1. Make six copies of the outline of the *Triceratops* shown here.
2. Color three of the outlines with a single color, such as gray or brown. Fill the other three with a colorful pattern that matches the jungle design on the next page.
3. Use scissors to carefully cut out each of the six shapes.
4. Turn the page. Scatter all six dinosaurs on the jungle pattern.
   Which ones are easiest to find?
   Which ones are most difficult?

Spreading Jungle

Here's a perfect place for misplacing camouflaged animals.

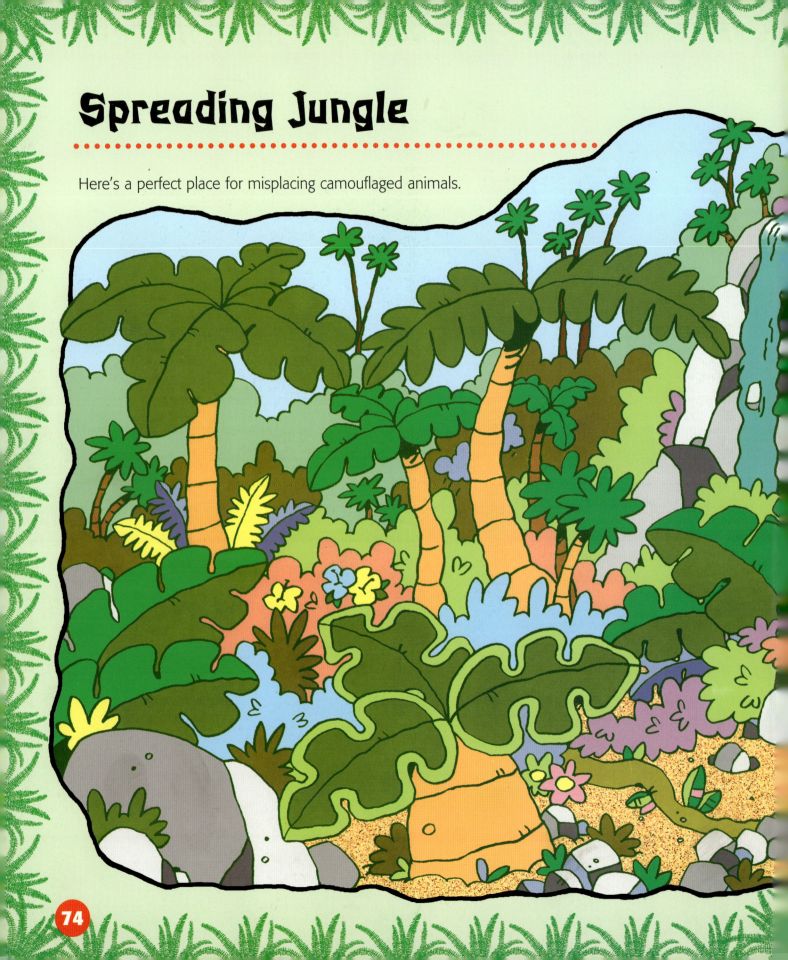

Wipe Out

And then there were none. No one knows for sure how it happened, but it did. In a very short time, the dinosaurs became extinct. Animals that had been around for nearly 200 million years suddenly and mysteriously died off.

Many scientists believe that the extinction of the dinosaurs was caused by our planet crashing with an asteroid or comet. As the asteroid or comet entered our atmosphere, it burned up. The ash from this blaze, plus the debris thrown into the air from the impact, filled the sky. The darkened atmosphere blocked out sunlight. Without this energy source, the temperature dropped and the green plants died. This started a domino effect that eventually resulted in the death of the dinosaurs.

THE BIG ONE

Although people like to think of the dinosaur extinction as *the* extinction, it wasn't. There were bigger and better "wipe outs" that occurred way before the first dinosaurs appeared.

The biggest extinction events occurred at the end of the Paleozoic Era. At that time, more than 95% of all the animal species became extinct. Bye-bye trilobites. No one knows why these extinctions occurred, but they seem to have been associated with major volcanic eruptions.

FADING FAST

You can model how plant life might have been affected by a meteor impact by doing the following activity.

You'll Need

Two small and identical potted plants

To Do

1. Place one plant on a windowsill. Place the other plant in a dark closet in which no light enters.
2. Water both plants every day. Try not to let any light "spill" onto the plant in the dark closet.
3. After a few days, examine both plants. What has happened to the plant that was kept in the closet? How can this observation be applied to the extinction of the dinosaurs?
4. When you are finished, return the plant that was in the dark closet into a well-lighted area.

As you saw, without light, the plant in the closet started withering and its leaves turned yellow. Imagine day after day of darkness. The plants could not survive. As they died off, so did the animals that relied on them for food. As a result, the larger flesh-eating animals—dinosaurs included—had nothing to eat and they became extinct.

Answers

BACK ON TRACK

The hip height of this creature is 50 inches (125 cm).

ONLY THE SHADOW KNOWS

1. T. rex
2. Triceratops
3. Pteranodon
4. Stegosaurus
5. Dimetrodon
6. Wooly mammoth

HEAD GAMES

1. Stegoceras
2. Dilophosaurus
3. Parasaurolophus
4. Triceratops
5. Brachiosaurus
6. Camarasaurus

NAME GAME

1. Tyrannosaurus rex
2. Pachycephalosaur
3. Velociraptor
4. Deinonychosaur

PUZZLING PIECES

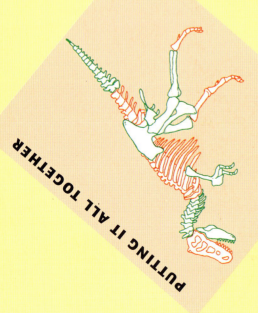

PUTTING IT ALL TOGETHER

KEEPING COOL

The cup with the aluminum foil strip changed temperature at a faster rate.

Index

About the Author

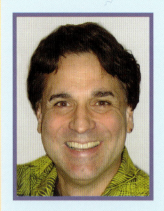

Michael Anthony DiSpezio is a renaissance educator who teaches, writes, and conducts teacher workshops throughout the world. He is the author of *Critical Thinking Puzzles, Great Critical Thinking Puzzles, Challenging Critical Thinking Puzzles, Visual Thinking Puzzles, Awesome Experiments in Electricity and Magnetism, Awesome Experiments in Force and Motion, Awesome Experiments in Light and Sound, Optical Illusion Magic, Simple Optical Illusion Experiments with Everyday Materials, Eye-Popping Optical Illusions, Map Mania,* and *Weather Mania* (all from Sterling). He is also the co-author of over two dozen elementary, middle, and high school science textbooks and has been a "hired creative-gun" for clients including The Weather Channel and Children's Television Workshop. He also develops activities for the classroom guides to *Discover* magazine and *Scientific American Frontiers.*

Michael was a contributor to the National Science Teachers Association's Pathways to Science Standards. This document set offers guidelines for moving the national science standards from vision to practice. Michael's work with the NSTA has also included authoring the critically acclaimed NSTA curriculum, *The Science of HIV.* These days, Michael is the curriculum architect for the JASON Academy, an on-line university that offers professional development courses for science teachers.

To learn more about this topic and Michael's cool science activities, log on to www.Awesomescience.org.